WRITING THE SIGNIFICANT SOIL

WRITING
THE
SIGNIFICANT
SOIL

POEMS BY DAVID ANTHONY SAM

WAYFARER BOOKS
BERKSHIRE MOUNTAINS, MASS.

WAYFARER BOOKS

WWW.WAYFARERBOOKS.ORG

All Rights Reserved
Published in 2022 by Wayfarer Books
Cover Design and Interior Design by Leslie M. Browning
ISBN 978-1-956368-19-2
First Edition Trade Paperback

10 9 8 7 6 5 4 3 2 1

Look for our titles in paperback, ebook, and audiobook wherever books are sold.
Wholesale offerings for retailers available through Ingram.

Wayfarer Books is committed to ecological stewardship.
We greatly value the natural environment and invest in
environmental conservation. For each book purchased in our
online store we plant one tree.

For Linda
who makes wherever I stand significant.

And for Dwight and Pat, friends for a lifetime.

For most of us, this is the aim
Never here to be realised;
Who are only undefeated
Because we have gone on trying;
We, content at the last
If our temporal reversion nourish
(Not too far from the yew-tree)
The life of significant soil.

T. S. Eliot

CONTENTS

1   Auguries of Ashes

2   Geology of the Blue Ridge

4   The Language of Rain

5   Angst of Sunrise

7   Red Clay Sunrise: Reflections on the First Year

8   De-Positing Truths

11   Genesis

12   Holy Unfirm

13   Murmuration

14   Sugaring

16   Black Bread

18   Echoes

21   Of Bone and Limestone

23   Shenandoah

24   Slouching Towards

25   The Frozen Man

27   The Burning Time

29   Two Children Threatened by Mockingbird

31   Couplets Indigo

32   Whittling Emptiness

34   Earthfire

35   December Cenotaph

38   Clinging to the Hillside

39   Refugee

41   Enlightenment

43   Words Written along Stevensburg Road

44   The Honey of Miracles

46   Meditations in Blue

48   Silence Lacks its Author

50   Walking South on Water Street

52   Nothing Like

54   Enlargement

55   First Birthday

57   The Difficulty of Morning

59   Geology: The Artesian Well

60   Peering through the Narrow End

62   The Naming

64   Taconic Orogeny

65   Age and Silence

68   Panoramas

70   Morning, Encountering a Snail

72   The Passive Voice

73   Still Life: Old Man with Mockingbird

75   Lullaby

77   The Numerology of Weather

78   Southern Wind

81   Prayer

Acknowledgments

About the Author

About the Publisher

AUGURIES OF ASHES

I speak the ashes and the water,
making ink from what has burned
and what has flowed downhill.
My text is the mulch of leaves
and the desiccated fur of fox
corpse along the broken highway.

Please read no hopelessness in
the suffering of what has past.
No life is lost in decomposition.

The pieces of atoms are eternal,
drifting into being and nonbeing
as easily as the sunlight sprays
across the morning dew and just
as easily across the red landscape
of the end of yet another day.

My fingers are wet and stained
black with the making of moments
into the tomb of cool memory.

Please read no meaning into such
peering at auguries of nothing.

GEOLOGY OF THE BLUE RIDGE

All these lives have become
shadows in windows of granite
and metamorphosed volcanoes
and the layers of sediment:
shells, bones and all that's left
of these ancient breaths that
cry silence and seas from old
limestone in their broad uplifts.

All that we are must some day
be such silent and stony memory.
All of our crow flying, our black
silhouettes in brilliant blue skies.
All of our black bear eating
of blackberries on mountain sides.
All of our doe darting from shadows
of cove forests, from maples
and beeches, from hemlocks
and poplars, from white oak
and red oak, from yellow birch
and buckeye. All of our vulture
soaring and scenting of death.

We who have eyes will catalyze
what we see in the memory
of such stone. We who have ears
will crack vibrations into the seams

of the uplift. We who have voices
will echo the morning mist as it rises
from blue gray valleys. We will mark
mountains with hoof, paw, claw,
scale, beak, root, leaf, hand.

We add to these mountains by our
bones, bodies, and all that is left
of our breaths turned briefly firm
before retreating to the essence
of our ephemera. All of our rutting,
our running, our waiting, our pouncing,
our standing on hillsides and valleys
at morning while watching new mists
rise from old memories of old lives—
all in the end return to the rocks,
Thus we must learn to read pages
long written in layers the Blue Ridge
have transcribed from all of our living
and dying beneath their shadow.

THE LANGUAGE OF RAIN

Rain speaks, its utterances
the spattering against the mud,
the meat-sizzle in dry leaves,
the crystalline descent of ice,
the roar of torrent and lash
against the fragile window glass,
the slop of falling water into
the sudden unstillness of receptive lake.

As I am unstill myself, I cannot
speak the rain, though I try–
as clouds unform, reform above
me in that wilderness of sky
where amorphous canyons mass
from unquiet air sated on unseen
drifts of water to fall in language
beyond word but heard by silent ear.

ANGST OF SUNRISE

Behind a wall,
within the underbrush,
across the vacant parking lot,
I know a shadow.

Something gnaws within
me, aches to scream
or at least to breathe
fire into the wind.

Below a brown horizon,
beneath quaking feet,
something asks me
for one of my souls.

Lying in trash can,
I find a dictionary
melted by rain,
words bled to oblivion.

Above the low clouds,
beyond the dead light
of the farthest star,
matters too dark wait.

In your hand lies
a warmth that nearly
heals me. I clutch
the veil of flesh

that covers bones
that name you
with the hesitance
of all life.

Shadows are absence,
not nothing.
I cast my transient
presence to their gray.

Within my breathing,
under the veil of my skin,
I contain amplitudes
echoing the fall of light.

RED CLAY SUNRISE
Reflections on the First Year

This Yankee come-here,
Virginian by opportunity and choice,
met the mountain singers
and the city music-makers,
heard the unvoiced despair
of poor hope in Richmond streets
and in shacks along hillside hollers,
saw the new ships building
in harbors where old
ships once brought crazy hoping
hungry pioneers up
the James River towards
Jefferson's westward vision,
Declaration of rising sunsets
carried by patriots who
cleared land and native peoples,
fought their own chains while
forging black hands to harsh fields,
met the descendants of history
and the new wayfarers
of Reston and Richmond
building business from
nothing and hard ideas,
remet the American birthplace
of Virginian legacies and sorrows,
and found this place of

red soil and lost tobacco
still ready for the passion of plows,
new order in a new land
where many hands can
still make Good Work
with our one Common Weal.

De-Positing Truths

October now, not Autumn but
what we call Fall in the States.
Literal truth in a word, but maybe more.
Capital "F" in Fall suggests the sin
of our conception, original stuff
that sticks to even us unChristians.

Then again, fall of leaves is not a fall
from Grace, but a fall with grace,
an easy drift of brittled racket
as leaves clatter against branches
already deserted by other leaves.

Falling into something less colorful,
a time of browns, grays, whites,
and the blue shadows of snowdunes.

Falling also suggests inevitability,
the demands of gravity we obey
when our walking stops being
a ballet of lift and fall and lift
and becomes an OOF against
hard stone and dry clay.

The wind speaks above lengthened
shadows, trees bend just a bit,
and a threnody of leaves percuss.

What if all the leaves in the world
fell at once everywhere, just like
that, no warning? Would earth
itself ring in some kind of knell?
Would a symbol become omen
and tell us it's way too late for
us to beg forgiveness of time?

The fact of today is dry leaves
descending with the sound of thick
paper being crumpled up and thrown
against a full waste basket.
October. Fall. One more time.
One less time. Literal truth.

GENESIS

A dandelion resurrects from where
I'd thought to dig out its existence.
Crab grass and clover overcame
the cultivation of fescue.
Tall wild blueberry and maple leaf viburnum
raise themselves into a fresh wind
from the carefully laid out garden bed.
In a world without judgment
there are no weeds–
just a persistence of flower and wily green.

HOLY UNFIRM

I pray to the near-immortal atom,
the one the breath Caesar blew
out from his knife-gaped lungs.
I sing the psalm of the cloud
of probabilities that shroud
the near-immortal being that
makes its way into the sacks
that bellow me past three score
ten to find a word for this morning.

We mingled things pretend that
winds are holier because we speak
them, that our sufficiency is more
perfect than the atoms that deign us
into existence. I kneel the knell
that gathers in a purple sunset,
contriving this day's name for
what walks in the shape of me,
and eat the eucharist of silence.

Body of world, blood of time.
I know that I am mostly empty
space, pretense of hardness,
made to be the delight of what
might otherwise have no knowing.
I sip an atmosphere of awe, taste
the insubstantial lip of all loss,
and rise to make my atoms ring
with the surprise of one true bird.

MURMURATION

Each eyes the nearest six
to gyre and swirl
then fall like atoms
in black thousands
to an earthly shape—

Then sudden stir again
and lift in swift wheel,
turn and dip
all golden-eyed
to spy a hope or fear—

A wave of feathers
breaking faster
than their sound,
their raucous
murmuration—

A single signal
becomes the whole
and drops again
to leaf black branches
just budding spring—

SUGARING

The tinny bang
of hammer against
metal parts the bark
into beginnings

that seep the bitter
into a steeping
fired by wood fallen
from these same woods.

If I could only tap
the bark to unity
and taste the syrup
of earth rains sun,

sugar seeping out
its unmeant meaning
from the slow flow
of this season.

But sap from the original
tree has sugars
written too thick
to taste with truth.

All flesh needs warming
thrice by fire and sun
and the thick turning
of tree blood sweet.

As hands stir the sap
of these waking trees
to an essence
of late winter.

BLACK BREAD

Black bread for supper—and the stars
in the water of the black lake behind
the porch of the darkened cabin.

Breadsmells play in and out the screen
door, knowledge of the oven. Breadsmells
play with me on the porch, brinked

at the beach of the black lake.
Recipe. Ingredients. Time and the oven.
The kneading hands age puffy, dough-white,

as fast as time darkens the rising bread,
the lowering horizon. The clock burns
the crust, but the taste is not offended.

Cut the crust, eat the soft middle
brimming in salty sweetbutter.
Cup hands for warmth around the hot

crust of bread, the night cold
with a wind from the black lake,
and water-stars quivering up close

to the shore. Got the time, the taste,
the hands to knead this black bread
of late summer, flour dust in my hair,

hands caked with dried wheat and dark
age spots. I curl against the chair
on the porch with a loaf and the slow,

insistent wind. Close enough, I read
the misplaced stars at supper—
a recipe of blackness in the water.

ECHOES

Morning mist rising
from the bends of the Rapidan
hovers above fields
that await their latest mowing.

The cool vapors drift
among the wilderness
of new trees, like smoke
curling up from fires

or drifting after being loosed
from cannon and blackpowder rifles,
their thudding echoing
in long dumb ears.

A fog bank forms,
a long gray line pivots,
then begins a slow march
into its dissipation.

A red-bellied woodpecker
calls out a mimicry
of long ended pain
now risen into the trees.

A phalanx of young maple
stand silhouetted
against the rising backlight
of the reddened sun.

Daylight exposes
the long ranks of tall grass
that march with the wind
downhill against the woods

as a flicker drums
assembly from his
perch high above the field,
taking his careful hungry aim.

A company of starlings
flash their blueblack metallic
wings and settle
hidden among the gold blades.

Virginia's clay was red
before these fields and woods
drank from the dying,
and is incarnadine still.

The Wilderness smoked
with gray mists before
the massed men fell at
each other in desperate lines—

as this morning smolders
with miasmas that ghost
the hillocks raised by
geology or long dead men.

The grasses and trees
screeched with bird and squirrel
long before last cries
of dying stilled into wind.

And the thermals high
above it all have always
circled in black vultures
waiting to memorize the dead

in their own flesh.
The mist has risen now
into a long summer day.
The wind has stopped

advancing waves of grass.
At a bare place I reach down,
and gather the memory of red
clay into my fleeting hand.

OF BONE AND LIMESTONE

I walk this low heaven of graves
of slaves and descendants of slaves
on ground they once worked
at the old Loudon Plantation
in far western Alabama.

The oldest stones wear single names:
Elizabeth, Seth, Jonas, Mary—
Bible names, no African names—
some so worn by rain and wind
that the careful etchings love made

have been sloughed away like
the rock surface under waterfall.
The newer stones have surnames.
But all are rough-carved with
the caresses of a hand's despair.

On the higher hill to the grassy north,
slave masters and descendants
of slave masters lie in their own
segregated disintegration under limestone.
Decay unites those never joined in life.

I step around these markers, fearful
of treading on the calm repose
and violating again those whose lives
were etched with too much violation.
The wind rustles leaves at my feet

and the wind cracks a winter branch
from a tall oak with aged joints,
a sound like a whip snapping.
Cold shivers me, the weak sunlight
unable to warm above or below ground.

Beneath these fades of names become
the limestone blanketed with leaves
and their decay, something remains
long past the end of all motion,
embedded in the urges of the earth.

SHENANDOAH

Sunset bleeds across this valley,
as once a thousand Yankee fires
blazed to ashes the hopes of grain.

SLOUCHING TOWARDS

Above the Blue Ridge
in a loom of western sky,
something flashes,
something thunders.

Below in the Piedmont,
maples shiver red
and gold leaves
in uneasy harmony.

It is the new season
struggling to be born
in flights of geese
and falls of frost,

while I clutch summer
to my words, then
speak them visible
for morning.

THE FROZEN MAN

God spared my eyes
so I could see through ice
and understand blue
it its deep manifestation.

I might have forgotten
myself somewhere beside
the road that leads towards
some Purgatory.

You voted your conscience,
and that was enough
to be betrayed
by the shadows.

Look at how my veins
and yours show cyan
through flesh that thins
with each living day.

You and I had time
but lost it when all
clocks rewound into
unhinged space.

There are black circles
around my inner sight.
That focuses me now
on what remains.

I live on this bed of ice
and reenact the moment
when everything stopped
and I heard silence voiced.

Pearls born from seeds
planted in oysters
become the way this
frozen man remembers.

You and I had no time
but found us when all
space rewound into
the black opal meaning.

THE BURNING TIME

The blackened woods
swirl in gray ash.
An untruthful blue sky
speaks a certain clarity.
The heat of our being
burns old redwood.
These most ancient ones
will live. They know
the fire from millennia.

But seedlings and all
that was rooted and all
that could not fly fast
enough have been altered
utterly. My forehead
wears a false blessing,
though it is a Wednesday.
I write the ashes with
my walking stick, using
no language but silence.

The soil has cooled.
The winds have abated
from the Santa Ana
that stoked fires lit by
a night of lightninged sky.
In the valley, a river
carries blackened detritus
towards the Pacific.

Fire has always been.
Here, fire grows with
the redwood, dies back
and returns another season.
But the earth is askew.
The fires longer, hotter.
And I have seen the face
of the unnamed roaring
in a fire tornado until
I could not look more.

My hands have washed
themselves in gray ash.
My sweat runs black
rivulets that unbless me.
The blue sky is empty
of any cloud or wing.
And I hear the portents
of the next burning from
over an unknowable horizon.

Two Children Threatened by Mockingbird

The picket fence hangs
from black frame as if a window,
swung left and lost to its fence.

      We see through two dimensions
      a linearity of blue sky.

She runs in pastel fear,
hair Medusaing to snakes,
while the mockingbird flies right
in trinities of abstract music.

The barn is a birdhouse grown large
enough to have a man for weathervane.

He points east at an alarm bell
shaped like a rail crossing light.

      It is perhaps the rising sun.

The barn's face is a corkboard
with a rectangular plate and butter knife
and a stick pin tacking nothing to it.

The pastel corpse of a deer
lies partially covered as if in a crime scene.

We see by no dimensions what
isn't there but dreams us mirrored here.

—

After the Painting "Two Children Are Threatened by a Nightingale"
by Max Ernst

COUPLETS INDIGO

I speak the dank mist
beyond the will of wind.

Near shadows, a Shiva of sunset
destroys the last of this day.

Night is good for unseeing
a way from home.

I must atone for my vanishing
before I can hear again.

WHITTLING EMPTINESS

Whittling on the cabin porch,
he watches his familiar hands
flick knifeblade back and forth,
bits of wood dropping down to
the planked porch to lie there
in bright sweetness, woodsmell
fresh from the cutting.

A cord of wood chopped, a fire
built, and one day's walleye
filleted and dropped into sputtering
hot grease. Then, having eaten,
and the after-day drowsiness in him,
he took up a piece of white oak,
and began to carve memory.

He watches his thick dry fingers
come to wear the sweet wood juice,
the white-yellow splinters. He
knows these hands, their ancient
calluses, special scars, the twitch
of tendon and muscle, the bluegreen
of veins. Still they are strangers.

They work without his will
until he finishes, stands, throws
the small abstract of wood,
his hands' sculpture, across
juiceless untreed fields, scrapes
up the splinters left behind
and saves them for the fire.

EARTHFIRE

Dry fog dreams
twilight shadows that die.
Dark and green fires
this red land.

Dig bright under mist.
Confound the luminous.
Cover any wavering awake
on the empty edge.

Here the end way
splinters beyond the hard,
yellows divine air
into its wavering.

Trusting the intangible
to another country,
nothing times strange
chances into not knowing.

December Cenotaph

"I am old, but not yet so old I cannot burn,"
he says, watching as the fire of his memory
flares with the sap still left in dry wood.

"I have been ice before, had to make heat from
the deadwood gathered from under snow, had
to blow all my insides out into a small hope
of flame that one match had started in browned
moss, while my winds were strong with winter."

He tries to bank embers of younger lust to glow,
but something cold blows through him, and the weak
flames shudder like a candle about to go out.

"I'm not certain how my mind has taken me
down paths I thought I knew, but turned out
wrong when I walked them again today. These
twists in the way seem to break the pieces
of my remembering like the sunlight fractured
by the slow turning of leaves in the wind."

He stubs his boot into the soil around the fire,
loosing sparks, sending one pebble into the heat
where it sizzles, then bursts with a crack as
all the juices it had sucked in from the earth
were released into the air.

"My mind is a slow cinema, a herky-jerky
silent movie with frames melted by too much
focus on one scene that should have been
edited away long ago."

He tastes the black blood as he swallowed it back
into his bile, shivering like the boy of seventeen
desperate to love a girl in the clumsy back seat
of his father's blue Ford.

"We should have run naked downhill, grabbed
the vine and swung out to fall into the old pond.
That's what I want to remember, not the fear,
not the waiting alone, not the awful betrayal
of every urge inside."

Once, he did swing out after the high hot sun,
didn't he? He did fall to shatter the quiet pond,
sending a flurry of frogs splatting from sunning logs
into the greenish cool water.

"See, yes, yes, I did once burn, I still can burn."
He hugs his arms around the coldness
of the winter day, watching the fire weakly wavering
in this bare spot amid the drifts of powdered snow.

"I'd hate to think my fire went out that summer.
I'd hate to think decades of wanting a different
August have damped me so I can't remember
how to start a scratch fire."

He smiles, remembering or making a memory–
it really doesn't matter. A boy walked naked from
the water, hand in hand with bare love, and she
smiled bright with her evanescent youth, kissed
him there on the bank before they went back
to the promise of the Ford's comfortable back seat.

"See, see. I still burn." The fire at his feet flicks
sparks of hissing wet wood as he hugged life from his
wavering memory. He sits still on a cold log, waiting
to see if a chickadee will settle from its chattering perch
to eat the seeds he's laid on a bare stone beside him.

Clinging to the Hillside

How sudden
I am elder, wizened,
faced by this mirror
of wrinkled, weathered bark–

one scrub pine,
gnarled into cold rockface,
surviving on snow melting
as shadows unveil lean sunlight.

REFUGEE

The rushing roar had thrown him joyous
against the seatback and he had giddyed
upwards after too long earthbound.
Now there was just the steady hiss of air
and vibration of engines as the Boeing
carried him in cramped near sleep
above the boiling white clouds.

Nothing to do or be tomorrow or
now for that matter. He could not even
read his future in *Sky Magazine* because
it was quarantined with his life. And so,
he took the sacrament of water and peanuts,
praying to voices that rehearsed his memories
into the latest version of himself.

Place your seatbacks to their upright
positions and lock your tray tables
as we make ready to land. Make ready
for gravity to return him to his place.
Make ready to untwist himself from
the discomfort of pristine blue sky
and unpadded coach window seat.

He had to have a new name now that
his future had been smuggled aloft.

He had to write a soliloquy in darkness
because his passport was unstamped.
A dozen tongues unspoke his history.
A dozen pairs of eyes unsaw his face.
He carried nothing but an empty brief,

and sang the prayer to an empty place
where God gave little souls one shadow.

ENLIGHTENMENT

Among deceits
of evergreen sameness,
a blazing maple
undulls my eyes.

How many leaves
have I missed
by the blurs
of my quick days.

How an ice fog
has silvered the dry
grass and every
leaf of my hair.

My lungs fill
with such cold
knowing in aromas
of a dying season.

My heart thuds
against the barrier
of the careful
cage of my ribs.

Scarlet maple
leaves rustle in wind
that unhoars them,
some dropping away.

I am motionless
and calm, awake
for a few minutes
in this new dawn.

WORDS WRITTEN
ALONG STEVENSBURG ROAD

On either side of this bend
of Stevensburg Road, green
stalks of corn rise from what had
been winter-browned earth.

Sometime last Spring, some
farmer in his Deere has passed,
mostly unseen, sowing rows
to pregnancy and birth,

then awaited summer skies
to descend in rain, fearing
droughts or floods, but ever
faithful to the soil he has laid

his futures in. And now, in
August, these stalks have risen
high green walls along a road
I know only by the juddering

of tires and wheel under my hand.
Tall prayers of farmer's hopes
rise high. Soon he will wend rows
reaping low, leaving little behind

for descents of hungry geese but
stray kernels and dry stubbles
where winds blow white winter
rippling waves of furrowed snow.

THE HONEY OF MIRACLES

Sudden in the lawn among the clover
that ferals the tamed fescue
despite all my efforts at suburbia,
a hum of honeybees, those I had
thought surrendered to the blight
and poisons applied like children's
angry sticks to every wild bloom.

Where do they come from?
There are no beekeepers here
in this world-part once farmed, now
grazed by lawn-cutting companies
hired to harvest noise and fumes.
Yet these few bees still labor to fill
their leg sacks to yellow bulging.

Once in summers sacred in eternal
brevity between school years, I
lived in allergic fear of bee stingers.
Now that I am peaceful to the bees,
they are lost to lice and viruses,
colonies collapsed like civilizations.
All gone like those fragile seasons.

I marvel when I open a new jar
of clover honey at the sweetness,
the aroma of open fields and flowers,

the memories of honey drizzled
on my morning toast by mother hand.
How empty will the silence be
when flowerless fields fly beeless.

I step down from this northwest
facing porch to study the buzz up
close, the careful toil from bud
to bud, the visible invisibility
of hovering wings, the promise
of taking the ore of all these petals
and miracling it to honey gold.

I am too far from memory's fields,
too near the earth I will become
to celebrate this mass of simple
transmutation. And yet
I do become the hope of honey
simple from the whir of wings
and buzz of bees who hive home.

MEDITATIONS IN BLUE

Starling chick in the brush.
Starling hen in the tree top
chittering a warning.
The haze above the cottonfields.
The steady heat and hot wind
off the Gulf.
Mediation in blue
summer heat.

*

How is it that a thought
can be forgotten and refound
in the maze of mind?
How is it that we can die
for a moment, and be
revived, and still
recall ourselves to us?
How is it that semen and eggs
can be frozen and unthawed
into a child that knows
us by our genes?
Immortality intimated?
Mere bacteria can go dormant
for centuries, and revive
when the heat and water
are right again. Is the soul
less blessed than these?

*

The starling carries its species
history in its feathers.
The chick knows to fledge.
The hen knows to fear and watch.
The heat blows in from the Gulf,
shimmering the air.
Meditations in blue
hot summer, awaiting life.

SILENCE LACKS ITS AUTHOR

High July drought, curl up with
the dry brown grasses,
texture the blades like false green
in an Easter basket of memory.
My feet will crisp each step
with the gingerly toe of an ancient child
towards the empty birdbath.

Now, as sudden as silence,
I pray the fall of rain,
the snake of liquid through garden
filling the absences with skies of puddles.

Make sense of me and these dramas
of recurring seasons when such
finalities of a mother's death
and a sister's cancer
poison my eyes like the chemo
sipped through brittle veins
into mists of falling hair.
Wordless me into understanding
worded things.

He said the world wanted an author,
a will to plot itself
the right characters in scenes
for some good reason.

Something may want authorship.
But it is not the world.
Something in me signifies
the accidents of every solitary,
inessential moment.

Wizard this man behind a curtain
of words and philosophies.
We are the tellers of our selves
in stories that fade, smoke rising
from the burning of leaves
incensed towards gods
 of drought and pain.

My steps crunch dryness
in incantations that beg
for a guttering storm
to carry summer into its leaving.
Swim me into such wealth of water.
I pray with watering can
as birds answer an empty sky
in silences of falling flight.

Walking South on Water Street

You would want me now
to walk these snow-drifted streets
in Saugatuck by Lake Michigan,
arm in arm with comfort.

The northwest wind burns
through our parkas and gloves
and layers of clothes.
Stores are closing, but
we need, want nothing
except this bitter clarity.

For the first time, as we bow
ourselves against the cold,
for the first time this long winter
in this long year of loss,
I begin to feel the rise
of inexplicable joy again.

You would want me now
to cry tears only because
of this harsh, cold wind,
letting go the sorrow
into the gray monochrome of time.

More doors close, more store lights
dim into the reflections
of the Christmas lights.
Yes, she is with me and I am content.
No, I have not forgotten.

NOTHING LIKE

An old fool
painting the same trees
with river colors,

expecting frost
in his eyes
to melt like sunrise.

I wave at green
as it passes me by,
a bus too full.

Yes, I can wash
my own self
like my own clothes,

iron wrinkles
out of memories
and weariness.

And I can cook
a table of words
into a mean stew.

My eyesight fades
with shortened days
this end September.

Ready or not,
allee infree and
strolling home,

all the time
in the world's
great remainder

lies in my bones,
white rocks
ready to be reinterred.

I am okay with that,
like any fool
motleyed by life.

ENLARGEMENT

The Brownie
had been posed
in the darkness,
set on the brittle grass
wet with dew
upright,
its black circled lens
eyeing upwards,
its gray, ribbed shutter
depressed and locked,
silence unphotographed
around it.

Now, the film removed,
unspooled in light
as red as sunset,
transmuted by baths
of acrid chemistry
into a negative
of things heaven-held,
I aim fresh light
through the enlarger
and watch
the circling streaks of stars
find frozen motion.

First Birthday

This is your first birthday
since you stopped
being able to count.
You would have been 92–
not that it matters to you,
dressed as you are
in silence.

I would have called.
You would have answered.
We would have rehearsed
our histories.
You would have asked
for my help in solving
word problems.

I am back at work after
five days off
with the second a day
of Thanksgiving.
I am not yet ready
to thank the darkness
for your life.

Today, I began the purgation
that proceeds a colonoscopy.

I am a little afraid
of what hides in my hunger.
I am a little afraid
to wake up to your silence.

But today is your first birthday
and I have begun counting.
One, another, another still.
I would ask you for help
solving my problem words–
but your Crossword dictionary
lies underlined, notated, closed.

THE DIFFICULTY OF MORNING

1

A spectral fox
muzzles its meal
from the transfigured
roadside mist
gray in drainage ditch.

It wants what all things
want. A pause in the hunt
and run so hunger
can enter the body
and be fulfilled.

2

In the bitter clarity
that burns morning
with subzero cold
I wonder
where the fox slept.

I wonder where
the bones of its dark meal
lie scattered white under
the fierce powder
of last night's snow.

3

I want what all things
want, a hunger
to enter me, a mist
to frost my edges
silver with bright knowing.

I wonder where
the clarity of dreams
went as I lie within
these white dunes
of morning sheets.

4

A bitter wind sloughs
syllables of bright snow,
erases fox and bones,
effaces syllables
of dreams with cold light.

Geology: The Artesian Well

The spring wells out
of the hillside,
uttering history
in the flow of seasons.

It has known dark
depths of rock,
felt stone patterns,
deciphered lime
hieroglyphs no
human drew, and
swallowed all in
its Proserpine return.

Old songs have lain
in dark underlayers
veined by time,
waiting for the water
to dissolve its speech.

Then new lips greet
the cold water,
and drink its clear
mineral knowing.

PEERING THROUGH THE NARROW END

He shouldered the wooden crate,
carrying its weight, feeling its
ninety-degree corner etching itself
into his flesh as he walked uphill.
This is how, he thought, this is
right, the dark sky getting darker
as the nearly-new moon set west.

He heaved the crate from his shoulder,
cradled it like the coffin of a small
child for a moment, then–kneeling–
lay it carefully on the damp, cool
grass that seeped the dewfall into
the fabric of his pants at the knees.
This is how, this is right, this is.

He unlatched the wooden crate,
the metallic snap of each of three
hasps singing out against the song
of crickets and the tree frogs in
the copse that haunted the valley
below the knoll–a dark silhouette
of bare branches in black mass.

The tripod slid into its shape as
easily as young bones. He raised
the yoke, twisted metal joint,

leveled the legs in harmony with
gravity, and stooped to lift
the telescope up to the level of
the eye–this was right, was sure.

The telescope mated easily to yoke.
He inserted the wing bolts and turned
each tight, swiveling the instrument
until it aimed its way to the quadrant
where Saturn waited in the dark sky.
Eying the stars, he adjusted more,
then bent to look into the elbowed lens.

Twirling slowly the focusing knob,
breathing out the vapors of silence,
he saw the planet clarify itself in
sphere and rings impossible to bear.
It was now, it was right, this was
how to unsee what had been seen.
Leaving the telescope, he walked downhill.

THE NAMING

They called me from their
early garden bed
perfumed with jasmine and mint.
All around them, the trees rhymed
with every other green thing
and the bees
and every other winged thing.

They called me "Bird" and "Fox"
and "Vole" and "Trout."
I did not answer to any
of their names, washed
as I was in the song of wind,
the voices of sparrows
and crickets,
and the gyres of starlings.

I was distant kin to them,
but closer in relation
to the water and the lily,
to the sky and the cloud,
to the meditation of the stones.

They called me "Nature"
and "Force" and "God" and "Anger,"
hungry as they were for denotation.
I am not wild or tame.
I am not strength or weakness.
I remained as silence.

They called me in prayers
of chainsaws and flames,
tractors and plows and pavings
of ways that circled back
into the sterility of themselves,
erasing what did not answer
the names they called.

They called me,
and I at last came
when their voices were mere echoes,
frozen like fossils
in the language they would not hear.

Taconic Orogeny

The old geologist bends
to layers of time
exposed in steep uplift.
Removing earthcaked
gloves, he touches
memory in the strata
exposed by the rise
and ruin of mountains.

His own history ticks in
aches of calcium laid
at angles to his joints,
just as dying seabeds
layered this line of lime.
His blood tastes like
the metaled water that
bleeds out this rock.

The mountain wind
curls cold fingers of her
absence around his. He
whispers her in the names
of ages—Ordovician,
Cambrian, Proterozoic—
and time breaks
in thin pages of shale.

AGE AND SILENCE

Tonight, I heard the rocks speak.
At first, I thought it was the creek
rattling flat stones in its shallow bed
as though playing some game with them.
But creeks can't be said to play games.
And the stones were silent under ripples.

Then I wondered if it were the wind
using dry oak leaves and husks of box
elder catkins to instrument some song.
But winds have no intention in them.
And the song, if there were one, was too
transparent to come from brittle once-life.

I walked the path, creekside, my head
cocked like a cat's to discern the source
of sound, its timbre, its melody or meaning,
its faith–if there is faith in nightsounds.
As I passed beneath the basalt outcrop
which hung above the path like a shadow

blocking clean white stars, I heard,
distinctly, the rocks' voice–old rocks,
as old as rocks can be and still remember.
They had much to remember. They spoke
in tongues long out of use, foreign to
my quick new ears. Only the sadness touched.

Only the sadness of their song kept
me from shaking myself free of dumb rocks
speaking. And I'm not sure rocks would
have called it sad, in their dark pastness.
I scrambled up the loose earth of loam
and broken sandstone to stand as I had

often stood, on the largest rock that
jutted from the hill. There, looking with
a rock's eye, listening with a rock's years,
I made a sudden step backward from
the edge, and held myself within the dark
vein of sound. I lost the track of time

that was my heart, and disappeared.
It was not the consolation that I'd sought.
It was not faith that rocks offered
in the dark post-moon night. It was
not confirmation of my poet's ears
to hear the rock in darkness.

Not life and death, not age and silence,
nothing of any bright realities of thinking.
But still the rock made negative my nays.
And I was still as rock to understand.
Now, as I pretend to lay these words out
as if they meant the night, the path,

the creek, the rock, the shadows, the sound,
the stillness between heart and knowing,
I fall from the grace of rock-cast sound.

The rock was old, had memories of memories
to remember, had lived for so long in
silence that it understood by wordless calm.

It was a mistake, perhaps, that it had
let me hear. It was a mistake that I had
listened, however still. Then, perhaps,
it's just as well the sound lies wordless now,
like the windless husk of dried maple keys,
or the shadow of old stone across a stream.

PANORAMAS

My light year
times infinity
extends behind
in a shadow
from atop Old Rag–

The horizon leans
me vertiginous
into someone else's
dream–

Who is that boy
raking the creek
with a divining
stick
until it becomes
the Shenandoah?

Maybe he was guided
by too much sunlight
and burns now
with so much
that is red–

There be dragons
and a myriad of things
squirming at the bottom

of that water,
rich in a muck
that forgetting will still
from its roil–

I wake to myself
like an uplift of rock
that suddenly arose
from lowlands
to find it had become
this mountain–

Silence echoes
my repeating self–
as I have used up
every snippet
from too hard listening
in the sunset
for the music
of the spheres–

Morning, Encountering a Snail

The oak trees
have shed summer
in yellow, frostfallen leaves
that must melt
into acidic soil.

Spider webs,
that silk invisible
all midday,
quiver now with dew
into silver sight,
on architectures of leaves.

A woman walking
a careful path
does not disturb
these visible tents
of arachnid hunger.

She sings of herbs
harvested and drying
from the beams
of her gazebo,

then bends
to study the trail
a snail has written.

His sweet trace
follows the morning
across dry leaves.

Ignored and humbled,
she and the snail
pause in
divine stillness.

For this eternity
in a moment,
she forgets sorrow
to see the end
of the path,

murmuring
ancient songs
through lips that speak
the air made visible
by the same chill
that briefly stills
the wandering snail.

_____

after Lorca's "Los Encuentros de Un Caracol Aventurero"

THE PASSIVE VOICE

This trail walks my feet.
This wind inhales my breath.
This sun eyes into my seeing.
This black bear beats with my heart
And I do nothing
at all.

STILL LIFE
Old Man with Mockingbird

In mimicked threes
in flights of brown
and slate and flash of
wing white stripes
the mocking bird

high silhouetted black
against stark blue sky
calls and calls and calls
always in threes like some
sacred bird trinitizing—

I hear in threes
and recall in threes
and see mockingbird
feather and call
bird and bobbing branch

I am an aging song
trilled together
by the trinity of bird notes
my aches my sagging face
my grayhair whitening

my frame and flesh
thinning like hollow
birdbones—until
I become light enough
for heavenless flight

flitting my salvation
in white flashes from
blue sky to hidden
branch in three
promises of feathers

LULLABY

How the rocking of flesh to flesh
and bone with bone
sings to me when the sunset
dresses me in rose and burnt umber.

The crickets begin their mechanical song
and the bat suddenly gives motion
to the lengthening of shadows.

I hear her voice soothing me
as it did when her hands, cool
from the cloth of the cold compress,
caressed my forehead.

And I feel the muscles he used
to hold us in his arms,
the motion of his slow dancing shuffle,
and the vibration of his baritone
through his chest and into mine.

I know the rocking clutch
she and I made of each other,
slow subsiding after crests of love
as the dampness of our skin chilled
us into unyielding separate dreams.

And I hear my voice as I rocked
a barely shaped baby girl for the first time,
seeking an ocean's quieter soul

to offer as penance to the wails
of her wanting something she had
no way to word or sing for.

What gives sleep to another
from the gentle work of flesh and bone?

The crickets answer with dry-voiced legs.
The bats stagger their alphabet
of writing the night sky.

The night subsumes me,
and I am content that my motion
lies hidden in the dark,
but that it also moves a heaven
of brittle September stars.

Then, I feel the earth's vibrato
moving me in tide and turn,
singing with the creature voices
it made from rock and water,
saying nothing will persist.

But what a wonder to know
and hear with water memory—
and with my visible breath
whisper a transient hallelujah.

THE NUMEROLOGY OF WEATHER

The sunlight frees me
from the shards of myself.
What do I care if a star
becomes the nothing of its burning
into soulless dust.

My hand moves before
I will it.
Does it know me
before I am?

I ask the winter
to forgive my understanding.
Seasons
have no knowing
and I impose my fictive self
on snow and blue ice.

The numerology of weather
fogs me in tonight.
I tend the solitary garden
that grows between
me and the world.
The loam of leaving it
will be my estate.

I breathe from a time
when I will have no time.

Listen, the rain is falling.

SOUTHERN WIND

You work into my flesh
like a seed into soil,
fragrant decay of husks
to orange flowers
bright and drenched
in sugared pollen.

The red moon rusts
in refractions of sunset.
The poplars weep leaves
that tremble in your breath.
I am ready to be rolled
up in a new night of stories.

The white wind burns
from polar north
in blue words
I struggle to melt
into my meaning.
Winds from other quarters
vibrate the boreal light
that sings above my register.

You come into my flesh
with wraith hunger.
But you've come too late.
My soul is mossed
from facing north
in shadows of time.

And I have lost the key
that unlocks myth.

Without wind, I am able
to listen for the silence.
My memory chains me
like a bird captivated
by its own trills
in a hot afternoon.

Mosquitoes whine
the souls of the hungry
dead in winds
that snow petals
from the cherry.
Then a storm grumbles
over a mountain
of long horizons.

It's useless to complain
to gods of currents.
All things will never return
in any older form.
The winds carry
the atoms of other being
that the poplar transcribes
with instruments of leaves.

Without your wind
who will listen to me?

Turn, dear one,
and make rich aroma
from what I have leaved
in falls of twilight.

---

after Lorca's "Veleta"

PRAYER

The holiness came to me
in a brown-feathered surprise.
A Carolina wren clutching itself
to the window screen and singing
one foot from my unclenched face.
Then it flew to the lilac
shaking its purple fragrance free.

Filled with such scent and sound,
I unchoked my faith in words
held together by fragile music–
and my lips formed themselves
in the shape of a bird as the silence
escaped as psalm.

ACKNOWLEDGMENTS

My deepest gratitude goes to the editors of the following journals and e-zines for previously publishing the following poems, sometimes in earlier versions:

Aji Magazine: "Murmuration," "Of Bone and Limestone" Heron Tree: "The Difficulty of Morning," "Enlargement"

The MacGuffin: "First Birthday," "Silence Lacks its Author," "Walking South on Water Street"

The Piedmont Virginian Magazine: "Echoes," "Panoramas," "Reflections: Red Clay Sunrise," "Words Written Along Stevensburg Road"

Poetry Quarterly: "December Cenotaph," "The Frozen Man," "The Honey of Miracles" "The Language of Rain

Red Earth Review: "Nothing Like," "Peering through the Narrow End"

The Scapegoat Review: "Geology of the Blue Ridge"

Smoky Blue Literary and Arts Magazine: "Black Bread," "The Burning Time," "Sugaring," "Whittling Emptiness"

Vine Leaves Literary Journal: "Taconic Orogeny"

Voices on the Wind: "Meditations in Blue" "The Naming"

Virginia Writers Club Journal: "The Numerology of Weather"

The Write Place at the Write Time: "Age and Silence," "Still Life: Old Man with Mockingbird"

About the Author

Born in Pennsylvania, David Anthony Sam is the proud grandson of peasant immigrants from Poland and Syria. For much of his life, he lived and worked in the Detroit area, graduating from Eastern Michigan University (BA, MA) and Michigan State (Ph.D.). Over his career he has been a retail salesman and then partner/manager of a small music and electronics store, a college adult and transfer advisor, a student services administrator, a community college dean, a vice president for academic affairs and workforce development, and then retired after 10 years as Germanna Community College's fifth president. He lives now in Virginia with his wife and life partner, Linda. They have two children and three grandchildren.

Sam has written poetry and other work for over fifty years. His poetry has appeared in over 100 journals and publications and his poem, "First and Last," won the 2018 Rebecca Lard Award. Six other collections are in print including *Final Inventory* (Prolific Press 2018), *Finite to Fail: Poems after Dickinson*, the 2016 Grand Prize winner of the GFT Press Chapbook Contest and *Dark Fathers* (Kelsay Book: 2019). His collection, *Stone Bird*, will be published by San Francisco Bay Press in 2023.

Sam currently teaches creative writing at Germanna Community College and serves as regional Vice President of the Poetry Society of Virginia.

www.davidanthonysam.com

HOMEBOUND
PUBLICATIONS

Since 2011 We are an award-winning independent publisher striving to ensure that the mainstream is not the only stream. More than a company, we are a community of writers and readers exploring the larger questions we face as a global village. It is our intention to preserve contemplative storytelling. We publish full-length introspective works of creative non-fiction, literary fiction, and poetry.

Look for Our Imprints Little Bound Books, Owl House Books, The Wayfarer Magazine, Wayfarer Books & Navigator Graphics

WWW.HOMEBOUNDPUBLICATIONS.COM

WAYFARER

BASED IN THE BERKSHIRE MOUNTAINS, MASS.

The Wayfarer Magazine. Since 2012, *The Wayfarer* has been offering literature, interviews, and art with the intention to inspires our readers, enrich their lives, and highlight the power for agency and change-making that each individual holds. By our definition, a wayfarer is one whose inner-compass is ever-oriented to truth, wisdom, healing, and beauty in their own wandering. *The Wayfarer's* mission as a publication is to foster a community of contemplative voices and provide readers with resources and perspectives that support them in their own journey.

Wayfarer Books is our newest imprint! After nearly 10 years in print, *The Wayfarer Magazine* is branching out from our magazine to become a full-fledged publishing house offering full-length works of eco-literature!

Wayfarer Farm & Retreat is our latest endeavor, springing up the Berkshire Mountains of Massachusetts. Set to open to the public in 2024, the 15 acre retreat will offer workshops, farm-to-table dinners, off-grid retreat cabins, and artist residencies.